PLANET EARTH

Little Genius Books
Livingston, NJ 07039, USA
All rights reserved.
© 2021 Shoebox Media
10 9 8 7 6 5 4 3 2 1
Printed in Shenzhen, China, July 2021
978-1-953344-37-3

LiTtle
GENIUS
BOoKs

TABLE OF CONTENTS

The story of the Earth is written in its rocks.
This 4.5-billion-year-old tale is marked by major events
that left their mark: the ice ages, the appearance
of life, mass extinctions, natural disasters, and more.
These chapters in our planet's history
are etched in stone.

But what about the world today?
In this book, we'll take a look back at the
history of planet Earth and ahead to the
major challenges it's facing.

Let's explore Earth together!

THE HISTORY OF THE EARTH

How old is the Earth? That's long been a controversial question. Because the Earth's crust is constantly renewing itself, there aren't very many ancient rocks left to be found.

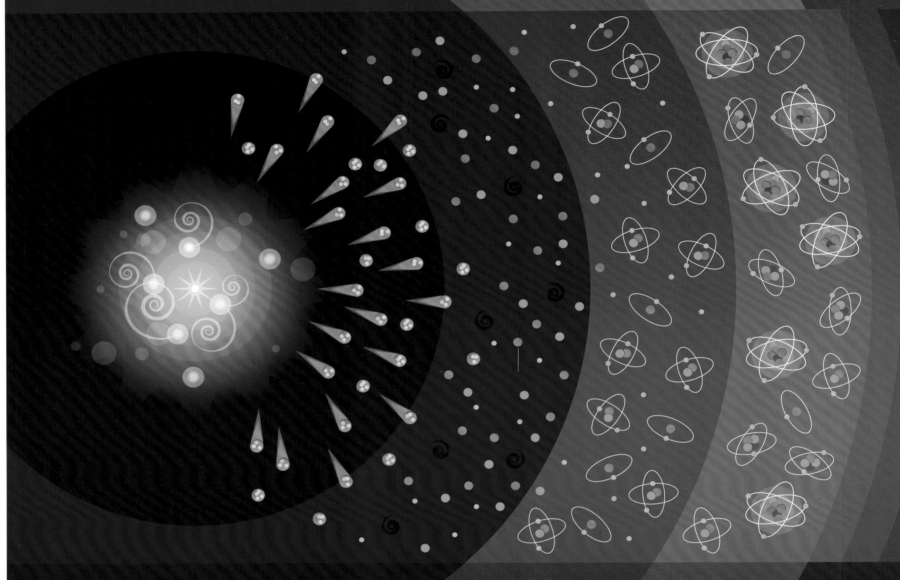

From yesterday to today

The Big Bang is a theory that explains how our universe was formed. Supporters of the Big Bang theory believe that the universe was once much hotter and denser than it is now, and that it suddenly expanded and cooled down very quickly.

Our Galaxy, the Milky Way, takes shape.

The gases in a nebula contract to form a star that will become our Sun.

FORMATION OF THE MOON
A protoplanet the size of Mars collides with the Earth. The debris thrown into Earth's orbit clumps together to form the Moon.

START OF THE LATE HEAVY BOMBARDMENT
Thousands of asteroids collide with the Earth and the Moon, some measuring more than 600 miles (1,000 km) in diameter.

EARTH'S ORIGINS
Several celestial rocks collide; under the effects of gravity, the debris contracts and melts. This phenomenon is known as accretion.

At the very beginning, our planet is a huge, endless ocean of molten magma.

Over time, the surface of the planet cools and a solid crust forms. The water in the atmosphere condenses, forming clouds and then oceans.

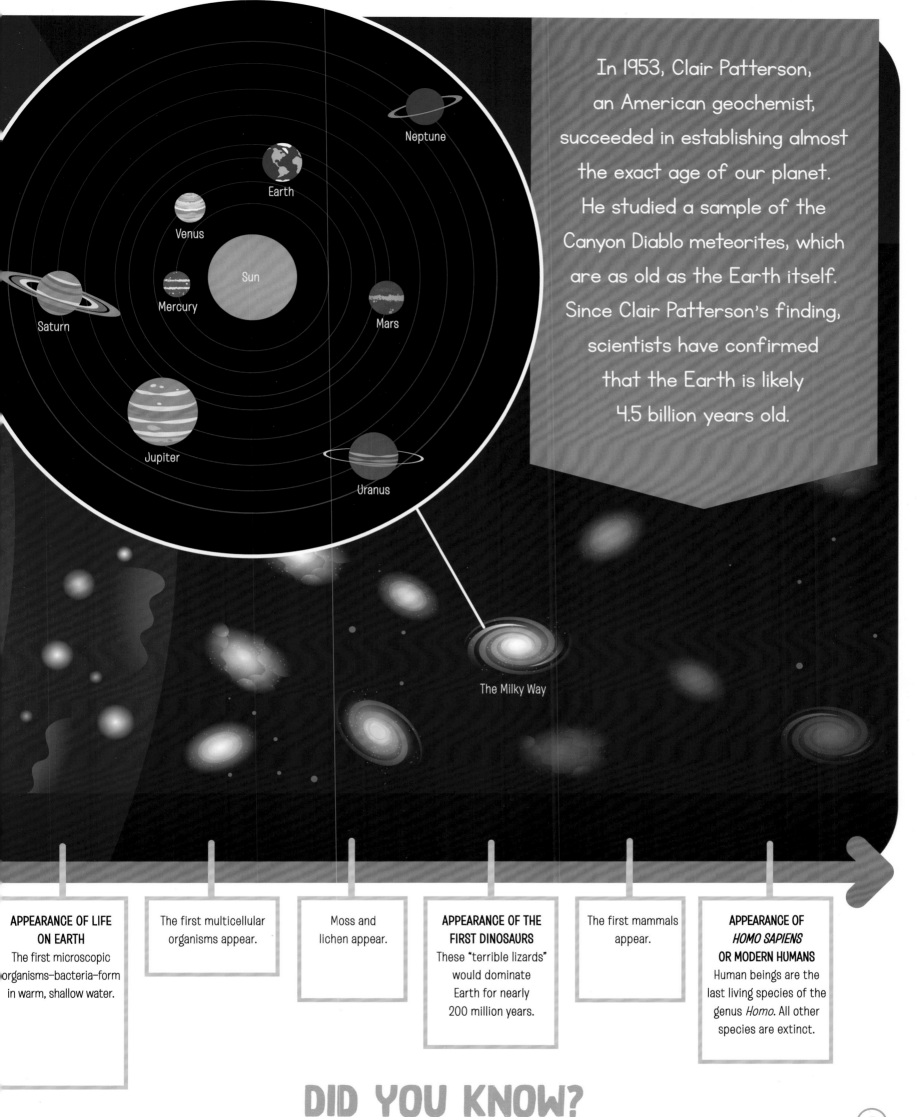

Neptune

Earth

Venus

Saturn

Sun

Mercury

Mars

Jupiter

Uranus

The Milky Way

In 1953, Clair Patterson, an American geochemist, succeeded in establishing almost the exact age of our planet. He studied a sample of the Canyon Diablo meteorites, which are as old as the Earth itself. Since Clair Patterson's finding, scientists have confirmed that the Earth is likely 4.5 billion years old.

APPEARANCE OF LIFE ON EARTH
The first microscopic organisms–bacteria–form in warm, shallow water.

The first multicellular organisms appear.

Moss and lichen appear.

APPEARANCE OF THE FIRST DINOSAURS
These "terrible lizards" would dominate Earth for nearly 200 million years.

The first mammals appear.

APPEARANCE OF HOMO SAPIENS OR MODERN HUMANS
Human beings are the last living species of the genus *Homo*. All other species are extinct.

DID YOU KNOW?

The oldest rock in the world was discovered in northern Canada.

THE SOLAR SYSTEM

Our Solar System is made up of gaseous planets and rocky, or telluric, planets. These are smaller and much denser than their gaseous counterparts.

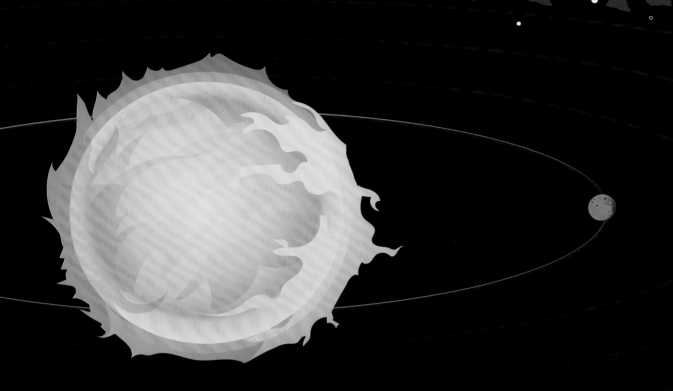

Rocky planets

Mercury

Venus

Earth

Mars

Planets not to scale.

Even though some people still argue that the Earth is flat, evidence proving otherwise has been around for a long time . . . More than 2,000 years ago, the Ancient Greek philosopher Aristotle observed the round shape of Earth's shadow during a lunar eclipse.

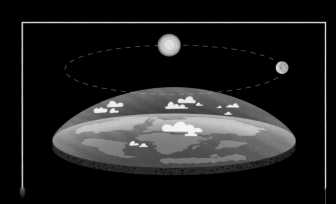

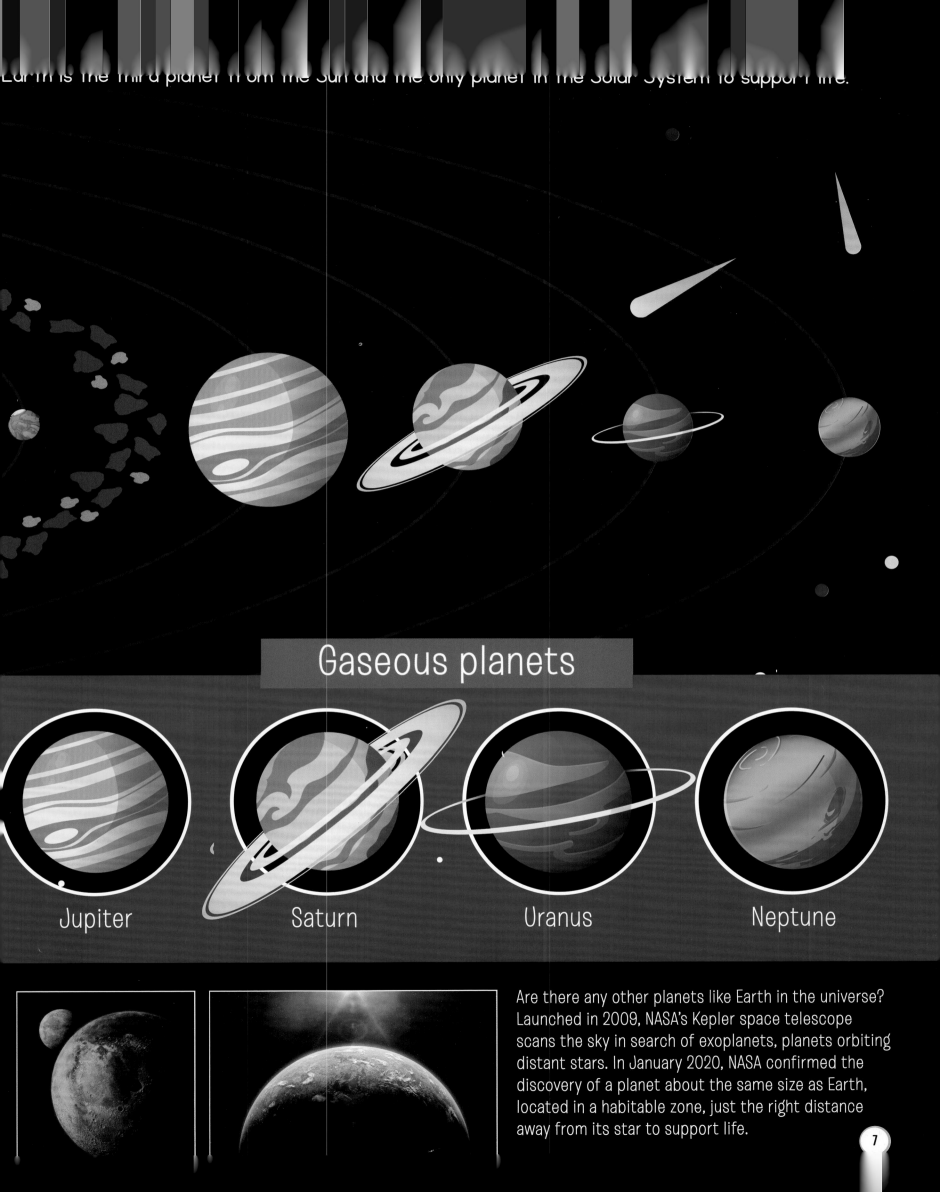

Earth is the third planet from the Sun and the only planet in the Solar System to support life.

Gaseous planets

Jupiter   Saturn   Uranus   Neptune

Are there any other planets like Earth in the universe? Launched in 2009, NASA's Kepler space telescope scans the sky in search of exoplanets, planets orbiting distant stars. In January 2020, NASA confirmed the discovery of a planet about the same size as Earth, located in a habitable zone, just the right distance away from its star to support life.

THE ANATOMY OF THE EARTH

Earth was much hotter 4.5 billion years ago than it is today. So hot, in fact, that the molten rock formed an ocean of magma. Under the force of gravity, the heavier elements, such as iron and nickel, sunk into the center of our planet to form the core.

1 **Inner core**

Earth's solid, inner core is made up mainly of iron. Its temperature is extremely high—nearly 11,000°F (6,000°C).

2 **Outer core**

The outer core is mainly composed of molten metals.

3 **Mantle**

The mantle is viscous, meaning it's not entirely solid.

4 **Crust**

Earth's rocky outer layer is made up of the continental crust, which is 20 to 60 miles (30–100 km) thick, and the oceanic crust. The solid ocean floor, which is only a few miles thick, is composed mainly of volcanic rock.

THE EARTH'S CRUST

Because the Earth's crust is made up mostly of rocks, its surface is very uneven.
The crust is divided into two sections: the oceanic crust (the ocean floor) and the continental crust (mountains, hills, islands).

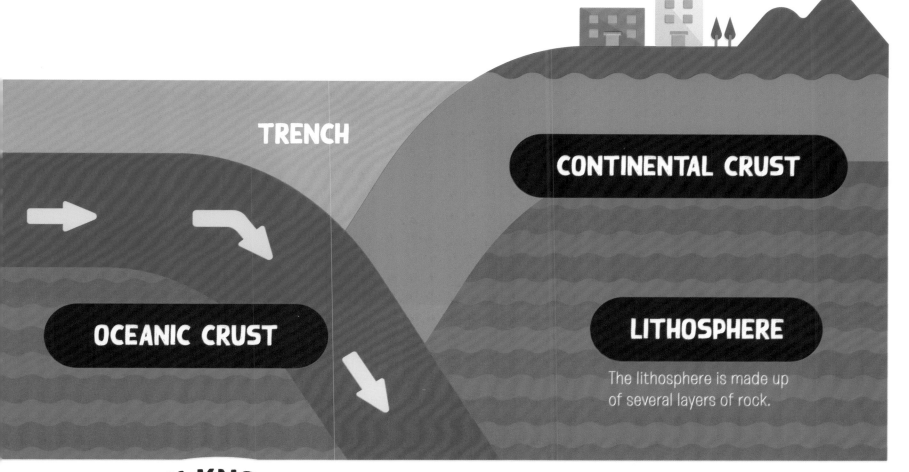

TRENCH

CONTINENTAL CRUST

OCEANIC CRUST

LITHOSPHERE

The lithosphere is made up of several layers of rock.

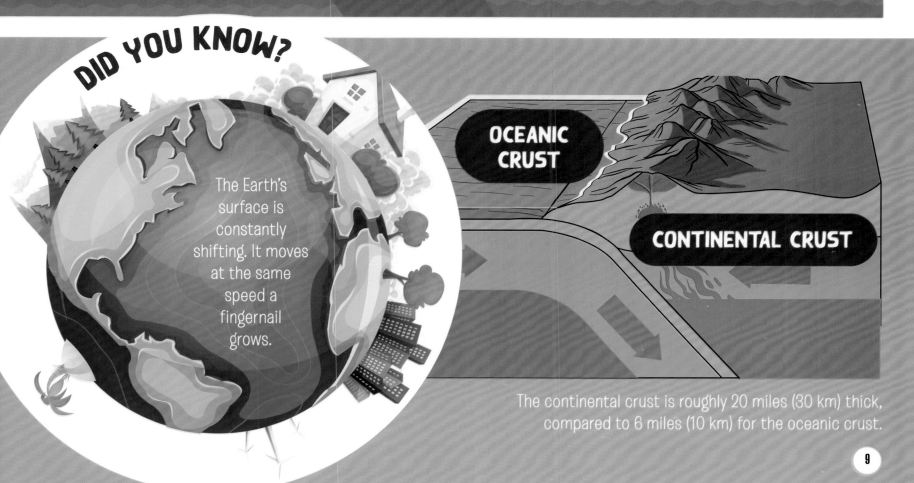

DID YOU KNOW?

The Earth's surface is constantly shifting. It moves at the same speed a fingernail grows.

OCEANIC CRUST

CONTINENTAL CRUST

The continental crust is roughly 20 miles (30 km) thick, compared to 6 miles (10 km) for the oceanic crust.

TECTONIC PLATES

As they cooled, the rocks on the Earth's surface hardened. The less dense material rose closer to the surface, while the denser rock settled on the ocean floor. The planet's rigid outer shell is called the lithosphere. It is divided into several tectonic plates that float on top of the mantle.

The continental divide between the North American and Eurasian tectonic plates in Thingvellir National Park, Iceland.

Most geological phenomena, such as earthquakes, happen along the edges of tectonic plates.

EARTH: A GIANT MAGNET

The movement of the molten metal inside the Earth's core creates a magnetic field around the planet. This force field protects living organisms from high-energy particles coming from the Sun. It is also responsible for a number of interesting phenomena, including the polar aurora, the famous northern and southern lights.

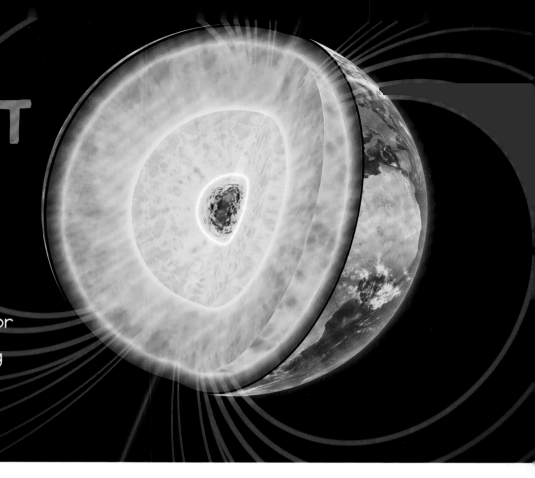

POLAR AURORAS

A polar aurora is a luminous phenomenon that happens when solar wind particles collide with particles in the Earth's atmosphere. An aurora is mostly green but can also be shades of yellow, blue, and red.

The polar auroras have different names, depending on the pole.
1. Magnetic poles – aurora polaris
2. North pole – aurora borealis
3. South pole – aurora australis

Polar auroras can be seen in several different parts of the world, including Alaska, northern Canada, Greenland, Antarctica, Finland, Norway, Iceland, and Sweden.

LAND OF FIRE: VOLCANOES

Mauna Loa, the world's biggest volcano, is found on the island of Hawaii, in the Pacific Ocean. Looming more than 2.5 miles (4 km) high, this volcano has erupted numerous times in the past 100 years.

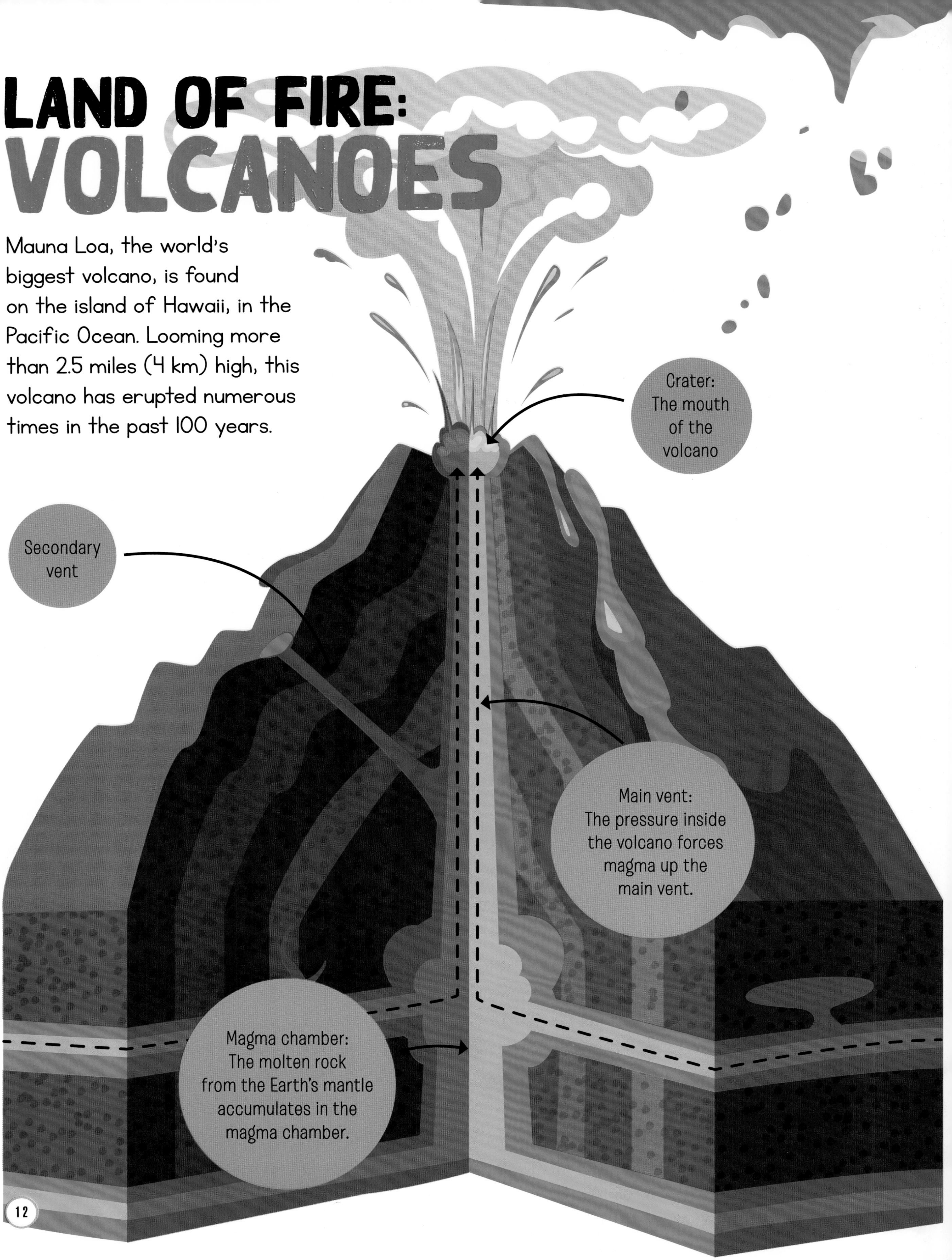

Crater:
The mouth of the volcano

Secondary vent

Main vent:
The pressure inside the volcano forces magma up the main vent.

Magma chamber:
The molten rock from the Earth's mantle accumulates in the magma chamber.

12

Almost 2,000 years ago, Mount Vesuvius, a volcano in Italy, erupted without warning. In a matter of minutes, the city of Pompeii was buried in a sea of volcanic ash and rock, killing many of its residents.

The ancient city was surprisingly well preserved under the volcanic debris. It was rediscovered by accident in the 16th century. Today, the site of the former city of Pompeii, with its Roman ruins, is open to the public.

Kilauea, a volcano in Hawaii, is considered to be one of the most active on the planet. It has been erupting nonstop since 1983.

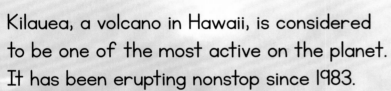

THE RING OF FIRE

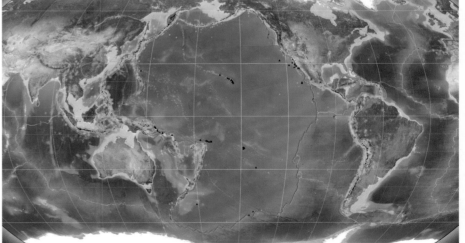

The Ring of Fire is a region around the rim of the Pacific Ocean where many volcanic eruptions occur. This path, nearly 25,000 miles (40,000 km) long, roughly follows the outline of the Pacific Plate. Earthquakes are also very common in the Ring of Fire.

EARTH IN EVOLUTION

The movements of the Earth's tectonic plates over the past few billion years have completely changed the way the planet looks, creating mountain ranges, carving out valleys, and causing continents to drift apart.
(Ma = millions of years ago)

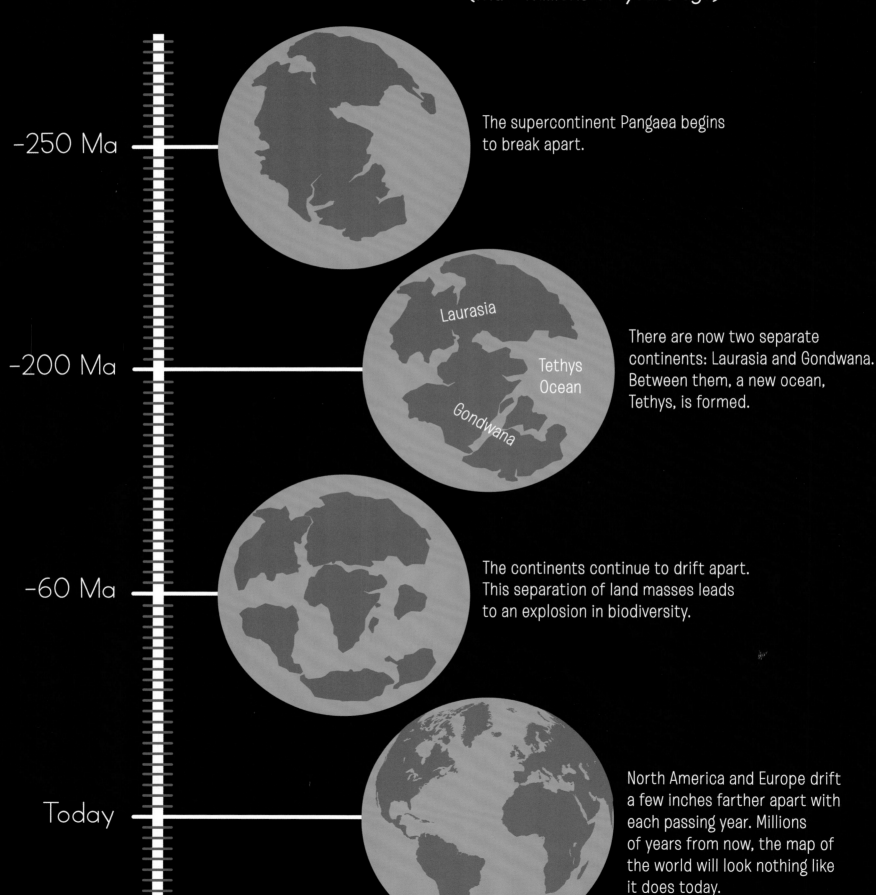

-250 Ma — The supercontinent Pangaea begins to break apart.

-200 Ma — Laurasia / Tethys Ocean / Gondwana — There are now two separate continents: Laurasia and Gondwana. Between them, a new ocean, Tethys, is formed.

-60 Ma — The continents continue to drift apart. This separation of land masses leads to an explosion in biodiversity.

Today — North America and Europe drift a few inches farther apart with each passing year. Millions of years from now, the map of the world will look nothing like it does today.

THE WORLD'S GIANTS

The Himalayan mountain range was formed by the collision between the Indian Plate and the Eurasian Plate. Even now, the highest mountains in the Himalayas continue to grow by a few inches each year.

TSUNAMIS

The sudden movement of tectonic plates under the ocean can cause a chain reaction of natural disasters, such as earthquakes, volcanoes, and tsunamis.

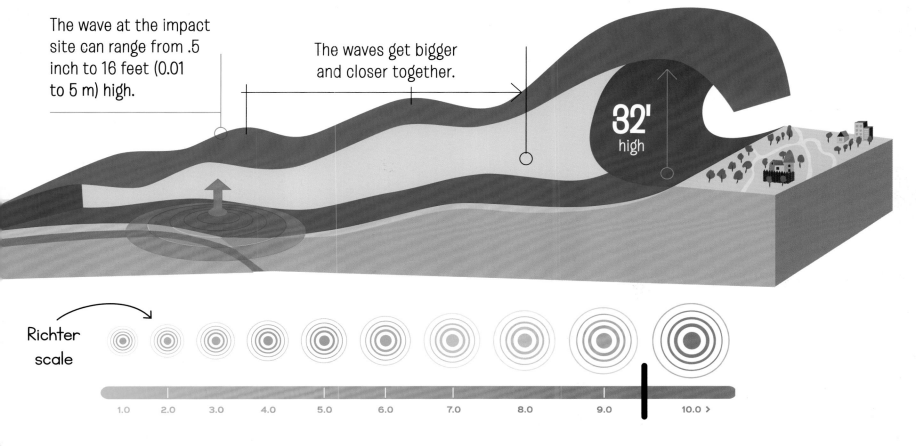

The wave at the impact site can range from .5 inch to 16 feet (0.01 to 5 m) high.

The waves get bigger and closer together.

32' high

Richter scale

1.0 2.0 3.0 4.0 5.0 6.0 7.0 8.0 9.0 10.0 >

In 1960, an earthquake measuring 9.5 on the Richter scale struck southern Chile. It triggered waves more than 32 feet (10 m) high that pounded the Chilean coast and swept across the Pacific Ocean all the way to Japan.

TYPES OF ROCKS

Over time, the rocks that make up the Earth's crust undergo several changes and are "recycled" into different forms. The magma in the Earth's lower mantle is the starting point for the rock cycle. As magma cools, it turns into rock, which can be divided into three main categories.

IGNEOUS ROCKS

Igneous rocks are formed by the cooling and crystallization of magma. There are two types of igneous rocks:

· Intrusive, or plutonic, igneous rocks form when magma slowly cools beneath the Earth's surface.
Examples: granite, gabbro

· Extrusive, or volcanic, rocks form when magma cools quickly on the Earth's surface.
Examples: obsidian, trachyte.

METAMORPHIC ROCKS

Metamorphic rocks are igneous or sedimentary rocks that are transformed by pressure or heat in the Earth's crust. Some examples are marble, shale, and schist. The crystalline formations most often found in metamorphic rocks like schist, gneiss, and marble are made of a mineral called corundum. Some clear varieties of corundum are cut into gemstones, such as rubies and sapphires.

SEDIMENTARY ROCKS

Sedimentary rocks are formed by a buildup of igneous or metamorphic rock fragments or other sediments. These sediments have solidified and transformed over time. Some examples are limestone and sandstone.

ORE

Rocks are often made up of different metals that give them specific characteristics. Some of these metals, such as iron, copper, or gold, are used for different things by humans.

When a rock contains enough of a particular metal to make extracting it worthwhile, the rock is said to be an ore. A deposit is a concentration of a certain ore.

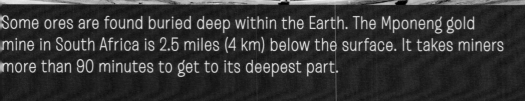

Some ores are found buried deep within the Earth. The Mponeng gold mine in South Africa is 2.5 miles (4 km) below the surface. It takes miners more than 90 minutes to get to its deepest part.

DIAMONDS

The elements in the Earth's mantle are subjected to extreme pressures and temperatures. Diamonds, a crystalline form of carbon, were formed millions of years ago.

During a volcanic eruption, diamonds can be brought to the surface in magma.

THE BLUE PLANET

Earth is the only planet in our Solar System where water exists in a liquid state. The surface of our planet is 70% water.

Water from space?
Scientists now believe that all the water on Earth came from the comets and asteroids that bombarded our planet several billion years ago. Because our atmosphere prevents water molecules from evaporating into space, the amount of water on our planet hasn't changed much since then.

MAJESTIC OCEANS

The Earth's surface is covered by five large oceans: Arctic, Southern, Indian, Pacific, and Atlantic. Ocean water is salty because the rain causes soil and rocks to erode, washing salt and minerals into the water.

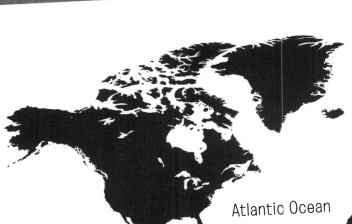

Arctic Ocean

Atlantic Ocean

Pacific Ocean

Indian Ocean

Southern Ocean

The Great Barrier Reef is located in the Pacific Ocean, off the coast of Australia.

The Indian Ocean is the warmest in the world.

The Atlantic Ocean contains nearly one-quarter of all the water in the world's five oceans.

The Southern Ocean was the last to form, when Antarctica and South America split apart.

The Arctic Ocean is frozen over for most of the year.

THE TIDES

The gravitational forces of the Moon and the Sun are strong enough to alter the shape of the oceans. There are 6 hours and 12 minutes between each low tide and high tide.

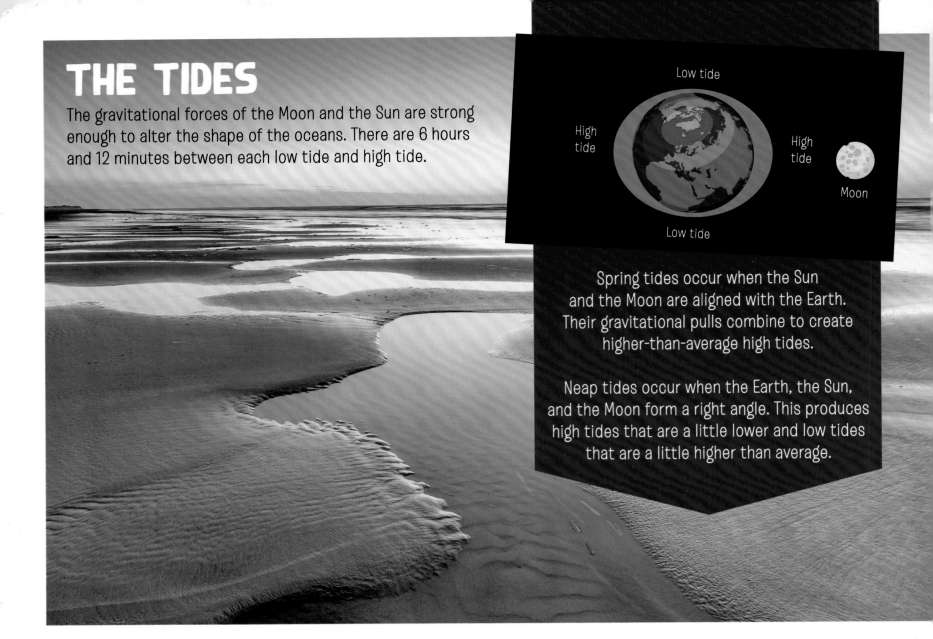

Low tide

High tide

High tide

Moon

Low tide

Spring tides occur when the Sun and the Moon are aligned with the Earth. Their gravitational pulls combine to create higher-than-average high tides.

Neap tides occur when the Earth, the Sun, and the Moon form a right angle. This produces high tides that are a little lower and low tides that are a little higher than average.

EROSION

Water is one of the causes of soil erosion. When water flows down a slope, it carries soil particles away with it. Over time, strong currents carve out valleys and create waterfalls.

THE WATER CYCLE

The water cycle
In temperate countries, people depend on the water generated by the water cycle for their survival.

1 EVAPORATION
The Sun heats the water, which evaporates.

2 CONDENSATION
The water vapor turns into tiny droplets, which form clouds.

3 PRECIPITATION
The droplets combine and fall back to the Earth as precipitation.

4 INFILTRATION
The water seeps into the soil, filling lakes and streams.

AQUEDUCTS

The water that people drink in cities is treated at water treatment plants. It travels to people's houses through a system of aqueducts. Wastewater is dumped into the sewers and carried to the treatment plants.

More than 2,000 years ago, the Romans built the first aqueducts to supply cities with drinking water. They used the natural slope of the land to get the water to flow from its source to its destination, a principle still used in modern aqueducts.

THE MERRY-GO-ROUND OF LIFE

In dry countries, water sources are often located under the ground. The water needs to be extracted using tools. Once these deep reserves of fossil water run out, they don't renew themselves. This manually operated water pump is specially designed to be powered by children. As the merry-go-round turns, it activates the pump, filling the water tank on the surface.

THE IMPORTANCE OF PROTECTING
THE OCEANS

The oceans are essential to our survival.
That's why it's so important to protect them and keep them clean.

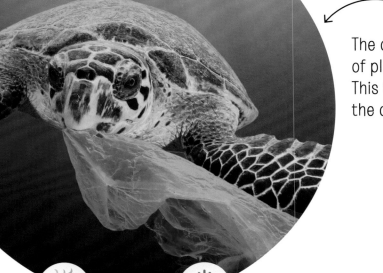

The oceans—and the stomachs of marine animals—contain huge amounts of plastic. Each year, thousands of turtles die after swallowing plastic. This trash poses a threat to biodiversity. That's why it's crucial to keep the oceans clean—to protect the plants and animals that live there.

The oceans are a source of natural resources, such as minerals, metals, oil, and salt.

The oceans release oxygen. Marine plants provide nearly two-thirds of the air we breathe.

Marine currents play an important role in regulating Earth's climate. They distribute the Sun's heat throughout the planet, which limits major temperature differences.

EARTH'S ATMOSPHERE

Earth's atmosphere is made up of a mixture of gases and water vapor that forms a gaseous envelope around the planet.

These gases are kept close to the surface by Earth's gravitational pull. They play a very important role in sustaining life on our planet.

Exosphere

Thermosphere

373 miles
(600 km)

Mesosphere

Stratosphere

53 miles
(85 km)

Ozone layer

Troposphere

31 miles
(50 km)

15.5 miles
(25 km)

THE OZONE LAYER

About 15 miles (24 km) above the Earth's surface, a layer of ozone protects living organisms from the Sun's ultraviolet rays.

In 1987, many countries signed the Montreal Protocol banning the sale of certain products that deplete the ozone layer.

What is the greenhouse effect?

Infrared rays pass through the atmosphere, where they remain trapped on the Earth's surface. This phenomenon is called the greenhouse effect. The carbon dioxide produced by human beings compounds the greenhouse effect and contributes to global warming.

In the past few decades, greenhouse gas emissions have sped up the process of global warming. One of the main gases responsible is the carbon dioxide produced by cars.

THE CLOUDS

When the water vapor in the atmosphere condenses, it forms water droplets or ice crystals around a tiny grain of dust floating in the air. Not all clouds look the same. Their shape and texture vary depending on the atmospheric conditions.

Cirrus
This cloud is made up of ice crystals.

Cumulus
This well-defined cloud is a sign of good weather.

Altocumulus
This cloud signals a change in the weather.

Stratus
This cloud creates fog when its bottom part touches the ground.

THE WORLD'S CLIMATES

A region's climate is mostly determined by its geographic features and where it's located on Earth.

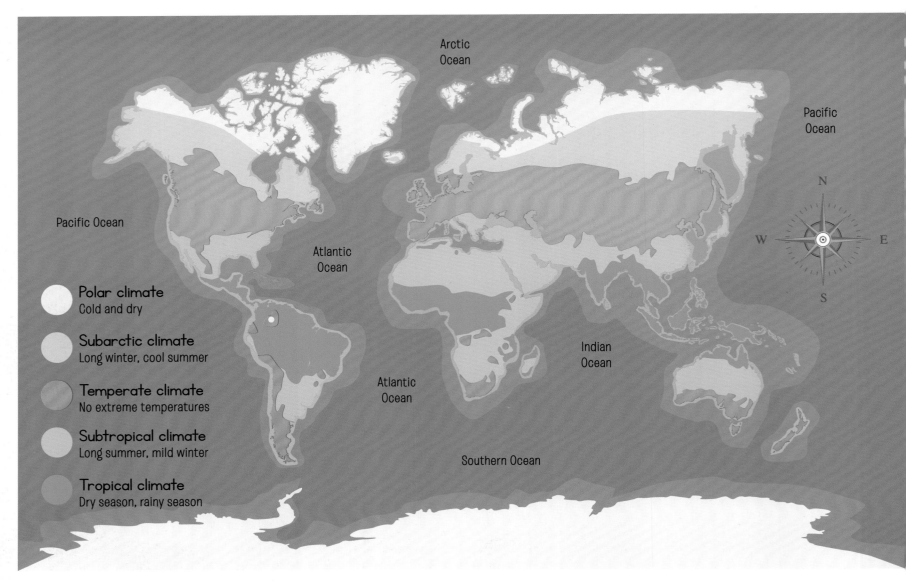

Arctic Ocean

Pacific Ocean

Pacific Ocean

Atlantic Ocean

Indian Ocean

Atlantic Ocean

Southern Ocean

N W E S

Polar climate
Cold and dry

Subarctic climate
Long winter, cool summer

Temperate climate
No extreme temperatures

Subtropical climate
Long summer, mild winter

Tropical climate
Dry season, rainy season

The seasons

Earth rotates on its own axis, on a tilt. It takes a year to complete a full orbit around the Sun. When the Northern Hemisphere is tilted toward the Sun, it's summer. At the same time, it's winter in the Southern Hemisphere.

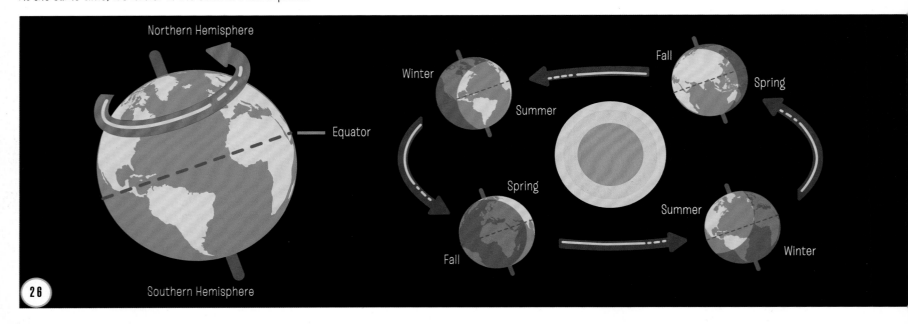

Northern Hemisphere

Equator

Winter

Fall

Spring

Summer

Spring

Summer

Fall

Winter

Southern Hemisphere

HURRICANES

Hurricanes are powerful storms that form over a large body of warm water. As soon as they make landfall, they lose strength.

The Saffir-Simpson Hurricane Wind Scale rates hurricanes from 1 to 5, depending on their intensity. Category 5 hurricanes, such as Katrina in 2005, and Irma in 2007, are among the most powerful storms ever recorded.

Since 1950, the tropical storms and hurricanes that form each year over the Atlantic Ocean have been named after people. This helps to tell them apart.

TORNADOES

These violent funnel clouds can travel up to 70 miles (113 km) per hour, destroying everything in their path. More than three-quarters of all tornadoes happen in the United States.

When a tornado forms over water, it's called a waterspout.

MONSOONS

In some parts of the world, the transition from the dry season to the wet season is marked by a shift in weather called a monsoon. During the winter monsoon in South Asia, spectacular floods drench the parched landscape.

WEATHER PHENOMENA

Weather phenomena happen every day on Earth, in the form of wind, rain, thunderstorms, lightning, and heat waves.

Meteorology is the science that studies the formation of weather phenomena and tracks their behavior.

DID YOU KNOW?

You can estimate how far away a thunderstorm is by counting the seconds between a flash of lightning and a clap of thunder. For every 5 seconds, the storm is about 1 mile away. For example, if you count 10 seconds between the lightning and the thunder, the storm is roughly 2 miles away.

10 SEC

WEATHER FORECASTS

Meteorologists observe, collect, compile, and interpret data on weather phenomena. Using measurement instruments and communication devices, they can predict the weather several days ahead of time.

The data is then transferred to a weather map.

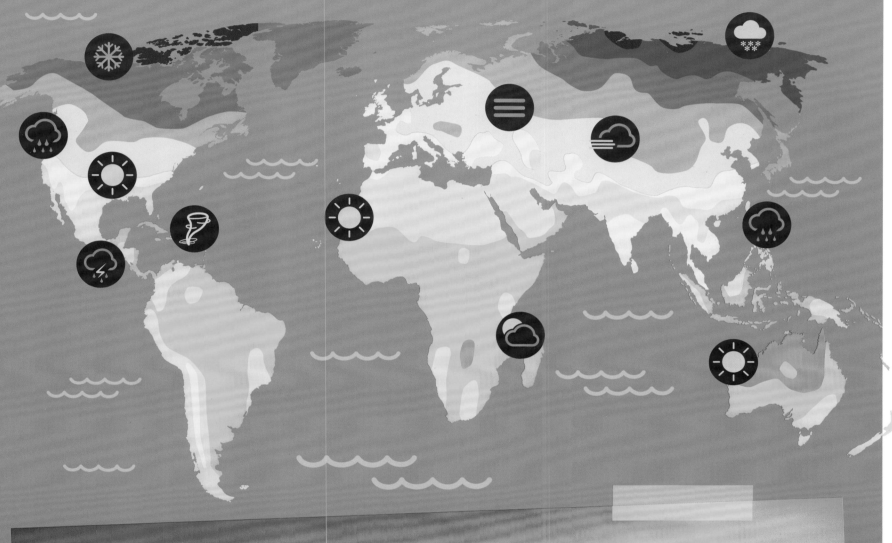

DID YOU KNOW?

You can predict the weather by observing things in nature. For example, if you see cows lying down in the grass, that means rain is on the way. And if the sky is glowing red at sunset, the Sun will be shining the next morning!

LIFE
ON EARTH

Over the past 4.5 billion years on Earth, millions of living things have appeared and disappeared. But how did life on our planet begin? Here are three theories about the origins of life on Earth:

IN THE WATER?

Life may have begun in the water 3 million years ago in the form of microorganisms, tiny cells that formed in the shallow waters of lakes and rivers.

IN THE ICE?

The first traces of life may have taken form in the glaciers. The ice could have supported the appearance of complex organic molecules, the building blocks of life.

IN SPACE?

The building blocks of life could have arrived on Earth from space, carried here by comets, asteroids, and meteorites.

BACTERIA

Bacteria are the oldest living organisms on Earth. Even though they're invisible to the naked eye, they are found everywhere: in the water, soil, air, and waste.

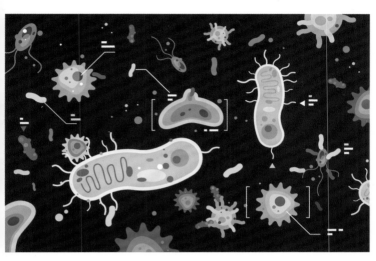

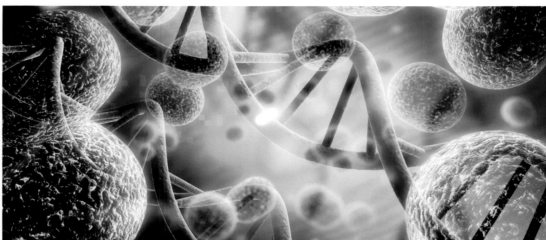

It's true that some bacteria cause diseases such as cholera and tuberculosis. But most bacteria are good for the environment. Some help to maintain our ecosystems by breaking down organic matter, such as leaves or the excrement of living creatures. Others play important roles in treating wastewater or pasteurizing dairy products.

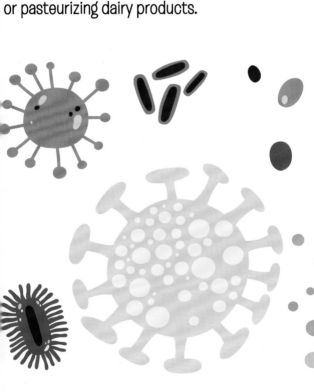

DID YOU KNOW?

A single bacterium can survive for more than 500,000 years. A team of scientists from Massachusetts, in the United States, have found traces of bacteria that are 600,000 years old!

THE DINOSAUR AGE

For 4.5 billion years, our planet has been home to countless diverse and incredible life-forms. Some of the most fascinating were the dinosaurs.

Dinosaurs appeared on Earth 230 million years ago. They disappeared about 65 million years ago. Scientists believe they were wiped out by a huge meteorite, which triggered tsunamis, volcanoes, and a dramatic cooling of our planet.

FOSSILS

Fossils are the remains of a prehistoric life-form (animal or plant) preserved in rock. Fossils have been found of bones, leaves, shells, teeth, and more!

HOW A FOSSIL IS FORMED

1. A living organism dies.

2. It is buried by sediment and decomposes.

3. The sediment is transformed into sedimentary rock.

4. The Earth's movements bring the fossils to the surface.

Fossils are studied by paleontologists. Based on clues, they can tell what species was buried in the rock and how long ago it lived.

SPHERES OF LIFE

The biosphere is composed of all living organisms and their habitats. The planet is made up of three spheres: the lithosphere, the atmosphere, and the hydrosphere.

ATMOSPHERE

The atmosphere is the ideal habitat for birds, mosquitoes, and bacteria.

HYDROSPHERE

LITHOSPHERE

The lithosphere is made up of plants and insects.

The hydrosphere is home to living organisms in the oceans and aquatic environments.

EVOLUTION

The naturalist Charles Darwin was the first to formulate that all living things on Earth have undergone transformations over the generations. This is what's known as the theory of evolution. Over time, new species have appeared on the planet, while others have completely disappeared. Only the species that are best adapted to their environment have survived.

If it weren't for evolution, you wouldn't be here! And many generations from now, humans won't look like you anymore. Maybe they will have an extra finger or their limbs will become stronger.

Charles Darwin

Evolution happens over many generations. But according to Darwin, the billions of species on Earth, living or extinct, can all be traced back to a common ancestor.

ENERGY

Since the discovery of fire, humans have become more and more dependent on energy for their day-to-day activities. Industrialization and global population growth have increased our need for energy even more.

In theory, the amount of energy produced should be roughly the same as the amount of energy consumed, since there is no efficient way to store energy.

Fossil fuels

To meet their need for energy, human beings have tapped into vast sources of energy under the ground.

Over time and because of a lack of oxygen, the organic matter trapped in the soil breaks down. A process called methanization results in products rich in hydrocarbons, such as coal, oil, and natural gas.

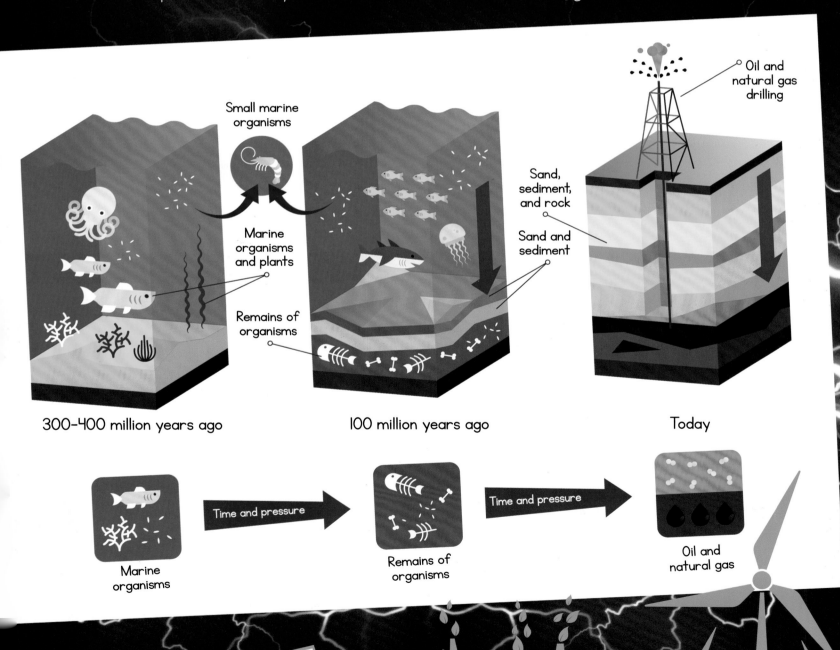

Small marine organisms

Marine organisms and plants

Remains of organisms

Oil and natural gas drilling

Sand, sediment, and rock

Sand and sediment

300–400 million years ago

100 million years ago

Today

Marine organisms

Time and pressure

Remains of organisms

Time and pressure

Oil and natural gas

ENERGY SOURCES

Because they take millions of years to build up, fossil fuel reserves are limited. There will come a time when these energy sources have been completely used up. These are known as nonrenewable resources.

So-called renewable resources are generated by forces that happen constantly or repeatedly. Sunlight, water, and wind are never-ending sources of energy. They are also known as clean energies because they cause less pollution than fossil fuels.

Wind energy

Sailors know how to harness the power of the wind and their sails to move their boat forward. A wind turbine, a tall pole topped with an enormous propeller, turns the kinetic energy from the wind into mechanical energy and then into electricity.

Solar energy

The Sun gives off energy in the form of rays. Tiny particles of solar energy called photons are captured by panels made up of photovoltaic cells and turned into electricity.

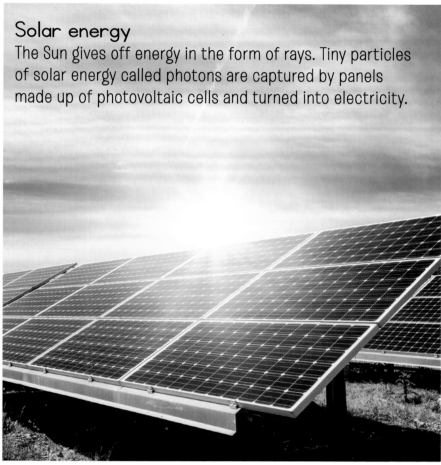

The law of conservation of mass

The 18th century French chemist Antoine Laurent de Lavoisier said, "Nothing is lost, nothing is created, everything is transformed." In fact, nothing is lost during the transformation of matter and energy. A hand moving through the water, for example, produces a ripple which, in turn, causes a floating object to move, and so on.

Did you know?

Northern Canada is home to one of the biggest oil reserves in the world. Oil sands are a mixture of sand, clay, and bitumen. They are extracted from the surface or deep underground and processed to produce liquid oil. The oil is then transported all over the continent through supply lines called pipelines.

THE DESERT

A desert is usually defined as a region with very little precipitation. There are deserts on every continent, even in the polar regions. They are not very conducive to life, even though some plants and animals have adapted to the harsh conditions there.

Because of their low humidity levels, deserts are great places for observing the night sky. The Paranal Observatory in Chile's Atacama Desert has some of the most powerful telescopes in the world.

The Arabian camel is an animal perfectly adapted to dry desert conditions. It can survive for many weeks without water. When a camel comes across water, it can drink more than 26 gallons (100 l) at a time—as much as a full bathtub.

In some species of desert ants, the workers store honeydew in their bodies to feed the other ants in the colony. Honeypot ants store nutrient-rich honeydew in their abdomen in preparation for periods of famine.

Some of the world's biggest deserts, like the ones in the Arctic and Antarctic, are cold! Like hot deserts, they get hardly any precipitation—no more than a few inches of snow each year.

THE TROPICAL RAINFOREST

As their name suggests, tropical rainforests are found in the tropics. This habitat has a warm, often humid climate and is one of the most biodiverse on the planet.

Tropical rainforests are home to many plant and animal species, such as the sloth.

Tropical rainforests cover 6% of the Earth's surface and contain more than 50% of all known animal species. They play an essential role in climate regulation and in eliminating the carbon dioxide that is responsible for global warming.

Deforestation is a major problem in the Amazon, the world's biggest tropical rainforest. Each year, billions of trees are cut down, and thousands of miles of land are stripped bare. Deforestation is a genuine threat to our planet.

Located in South America, the Amazon rainforest is home to more than 10% of the world's animal and plant species and to millions of insect species. This dense jungle still conceals many mysteries and undiscovered species.

THE TEMPERATE FOREST

In North America, the boreal forest stretches from Newfoundland to Alaska, covering an area of several million acres. This cool forest contains mainly evergreens, along with some deciduous trees.

The forest floor is the layer of organic matter found on the ground. The debris exists in various stages of decomposition.

The roots of trees and plants grow down into the topsoil. This layer of soil is made up of small rocks and organic matter.

Deciduous trees lose their leaves in the fall. Some examples are birch, oak, and maple trees.

Evergreen trees keep their leaves all year long. The dead leaves stay on the branches until new buds grow in the spring.

43

THE SAVANNAH, THE STEPPES, AND THE PLAINS

These vast, grassy, almost treeless expanses are a major source of food for the herds of herbivores, insects, and birds that live there.

The nomadic peoples who live on the grassy plains of Mongolia survive by breeding horses. Sheltered from the modern world, the breeders migrate from pasture to pasture, following the rhythm of the seasons.

The Silk Road, which stretched more than 4,000 miles (6,400 km), once ran between Xi'an, China and Antioch, Turkey. For thousands of years, caravans of merchants crossed the plains of Asia and Europe, bringing spices, weapons, and other riches, including silk, to the Europeans!

The steppes and the prairies depend on periodic fires to clear away debris and allow for new growth. These fires can be man-made or triggered by lightning.

The African savannah is home to a wide range of animals. The giraffe, ostrich, zebra, elephant, lion, and hippopotamus are some of the best-known species.

THE MOUNTAINS

There are many geological reasons to explain how hills and mountains were formed. It could have been a collision between two tectonic plates or a volcanic eruption. Either way, mountains are natural boundaries that appeal to our imagination.

Very few climbers can say that they've conquered the Seven Summits—the highest mountains on each of the seven continents. They range in height from 7,310 feet (2,228 m) for Mount Kosciuszko in Australia to 29,031 feet (8,849 m) for Mount Everest in Nepal.

In the Incan culture, each mountain has its own spirit or "apu," which protects people, crops, and livestock. Sacrifices were sometimes made to appease the gods.

A sherpa is a guide who leads a climbing expedition in the Himalayan mountains. The Sherpa are also a group of mountain-dwelling people in Tibet.

Golden eagles build nests up to 8 feet (2.5 m) in diameter. This enormous bird of prey sometimes nests on the sides of mountains. Year after year, eagle pairs return to the same nest, each time adding branches and other materials to make it stronger.

THE OCEANS

The seas and oceans contain 96.5% of the world's water.

The Sun's rays don't reach very far beyond the surface of the water. The deeper you descend into the ocean, the colder the water gets and the higher the pressure rises.

Ocean currents are caused by the dominant winds on the surface of the water and by changes in water density far beneath. Surface currents are warmer than deep currents.

The wind creates waves on the surface of the ocean. The size of the wave is determined by the strength of the wind and the stretch of water it blows over without encountering any obstacles. In 2018, a wave measuring 78 feet (24 m) high was recorded in New Zealand—the height of an 8-story building!

The abyssal plain, located at a depth of more than 13,000 feet (4,000 m), covers a very large part of the ocean floor.

NATURAL DISASTERS

A natural disaster is caused by a weather event, such as a snowstorm, a thunderstorm, or a heat wave. It can also be triggered by human error.

DISASTERS ON LAND

AVALANCHES

Avalanches can be caused by many things: wind, rain, snow, global warming, earthquakes, and even a sudden move by an animal! The steeper the slope, the faster the snow will move. Snow can travel at speeds of up to 100 miles (160 km) per hour!

WILDFIRES

Wildfires can be started by lightning, lava, or even the Sun's rays. But humans are also a major cause! Wildfires can happen in forests, woodlands, or grasslands. Not only do they kill plants and animals, they also release massive amounts of carbon dioxide (CO_2) into the atmosphere.

FLOODS

As natural disasters go, floods are one of the most destructive. They can be caused by torrential rain or earthquakes. Global warming is also a major factor. The melting ice caps are causing the water level in lakes, rivers, and oceans to rise. These bodies of water have the potential to cause tremendous damage if they burst their banks, destroying buildings, causing landslides, and even killing people.

OIL SPILLS

Oil is very harmful to ecosystems. When an oil spill happens, a huge, black slick spreads out across a big part of the ocean's surface. The oil destroys everything in its path, including marine plants and animals. The aquatic creatures that come up for air or the birds that dive into the water become covered in oil and swallow the toxic substance. Experts need to act very quickly after an oil spill to clean up the mess.

MELTING ICE CAPS

Climate change is causing the ice caps and glaciers to melt. The ice caps in the Arctic Ocean are melting at an alarming rate. If this keeps up, sea levels will rise, triggering more natural disasters.

BLUE-GREEN ALGAE

Cyanobacteria, also called blue-green algae, appeared on Earth about 3 billion years ago. Small amounts of cyanobacteria in lakes and rivers are not normally a problem. However, the pollution in the past few decades has caused them to multiply, endangering the health of marine animals.

OUR RECORD-BREAKING EARTH

The Earth is a very surprising place. Here are some of our planet's most impressive records.

What's the windiest place on Earth? Commonwealth Bay in Antarctica, where wind speeds can reach up to 200 miles (322 km) per hour during a severe storm.

The closest point to Earth's core is in the Mariana Trench in the Pacific Ocean. It is estimated to be 36,000 feet (11,000 m) deep.

The deepest lake on Earth–Lake Baikal at 5,387 feet (1,642 m) deep–is in Russia.

The coldest place on Earth was found to be in the middle of Antarctica, where temperatures as low as −148°F (−100°C) have been recorded!

At 4,350 miles (7,000 km) long, the Andes Cordillera is the longest mountain range in the world.

The biggest island on Earth is Greenland, with a surface area of 836,300 mi² (2,170,000 km²).

THE FIGHT
AGAINST CLIMATE CHANGE

These days, there are serious environmental problems threatening our survival on Earth. Scientists are sending a clear and alarming message: We need to change our habits—and quickly—if we hope to limit the damage. Global warming will lead to more and more extreme weather events.

HURRICANES

FLOODS

Hurricanes will get stronger and happen more often. Because the water will evaporate faster, the winds will become stronger and the swirling masses of air more destructive.

Rising temperatures will lead to more floods. The tail ends of hurricanes will bring more rain, causing lakes and rivers to overflow more often.

HEAT WAVES

With average annual temperatures on the rise around the world, heat waves will happen more often and last longer in the years to come.

In August 2018, the young Swedish activist Greta Thunberg staged a protest outside of Sweden's parliament building against her government's inaction on climate change. Her "School Strike for Climate" was widely covered by the media and quickly took on a global scale. The teen became the face of the fight against climate change.

TAKING CARE
OF THE EARTH

We only have one planet, and we need to handle it with care. The waste produced by humans is polluting our air and water. Our resources are limited, so we all need to do our part to contain the damage.

DON'T WASTE WATER

We need water to survive. A few easy ways to cut down on your water consumption are to turn off the water while brushing your teeth, take a shower instead of a bath, and avoid flushing the toilet too often.

SAVE ENERGY

To reduce your energy consumption, turn off the lights whenever you leave a room. Remember to unplug your charger once your phone or tablet is fully charged. And replace the light bulbs in your home with energy-efficient versions, such as LED bulbs.

CUT DOWN ON WASTE

It takes more than 400 years for a plastic bag to degrade! To cut the amount of waste you produce, use reusable bags and containers, bamboo straws, and a stainless-steel thermos or water bottle for food and drinks. Compost your table scraps. Instead of throwing away items you no longer use, donate them.

QUIZ

1 What is the name of the theory about how the universe was formed?

a) The Big Bang   b) The Big Tank

c) The Big Surprise   d) The Big Splash

7 What is Pangaea?

a) A supercontinent   b) A superhuman

c) A super mountain   d) A super ocean

2 How old is the Earth?

a) 4.5 thousand years old   b) 4.5 million years old

c) 4.5 billion years old   d) 4.5 trillion years old

8 What causes tsunamis?

a) Earthquakes   b) Volcanic eruptions

c) Underwater landslides   d) All of the above

3 What is an exoplanet?

a) An outer planet

b) A planet roughly the same size as Earth

c) A blue planet   d) A pretend planet

9 Which of these climates is cold and dry?

a) Tropical   b) Polar

c) Temperate   d) Subarctic

4 Which of the Earth's layer is viscous?

a) The crust   b) The mantle

c) The outer core   d) The inner core

10 Which ocean is the warmest in the world?

a) Arctic   b) Pacific

c) Indian   d) Atlantic

5 Where was the oldest rock in the world found?

a) Egypt   b) Mexico

c) Canada   d) France

11 Which science involves the study of weather phenomena?

a) Archeology   b) Meteorology

c) Medicine   d) Philosophy

6 What is the biggest volcano on Earth?

a) Mount Fuji   b) Mauna Loa

c) Mount Vesuvius   d) Kilauea

12 How long can a bacterium survive?

a) 5 years   b) 600,000 years

c) 3 million years   d) 4.5 billion years

13 What is a person called who studies fossils?

a) Paleontologist   b) Archeologist

c) Arborist   d) Architect

14 What sphere do sea turtles live in?

a) The atmosphere   b) The lithosphere

c) The hydrosphere   d) The ozone layer

15 What is the biggest island on Earth?

a) Iceland   b) Australia

c) Greenland   d) Mauritius

16 How many years does it take for a plastic bag to degrade?

a) 1 year   b) 30 years

c) 150 years   d) 400 years

17 What causes erosion?

a) The Sun   b) Heavy rain

c) Children   d) The Moon

18 What is an aqueduct?

a) A boat   b) A fishing rod

c) A coffee machine   d) A water pipe

19 What is ozone?

a) A bubble   b) A cloud

c) A gas   d) A crystal

20 What does the Saffir-Simpson Hurricane Wind Scale measure?

a) The intensity of a storm   b) The size of a cloud

c) The speed of a bird   d) The power of lightning

21 Which of these forms of energy is non-renewable?

a) Wind power   b) Solar power

c) Fossil fuel   d) All of the above

22 What is a characteristic of a desert?

a) It rarely rains   b) Life flourishes there

c) There's not much air

d) It's underground

23 Where are most known animal species found?

a) In Antarctica   b) In the tundra

c) In the temperate forest   d) In the tropical rainforest

24 What is the deepest place on Earth?

a) The coastal zone   b) The Himalayas

c) The Mariana Trench   d) The Montana Desert

Answers: 1. a), 2. c), 3. a), 4. b), 5. c), 6. b), 7. a), 8. d), 9. b), 10. c), 11. b), 12. b), 13. a), 14. c), 15. c), 16. d), 17. b), 18. d), 19. c), 20. a), 21. c), 22. a), 23. d), 24. c)

59

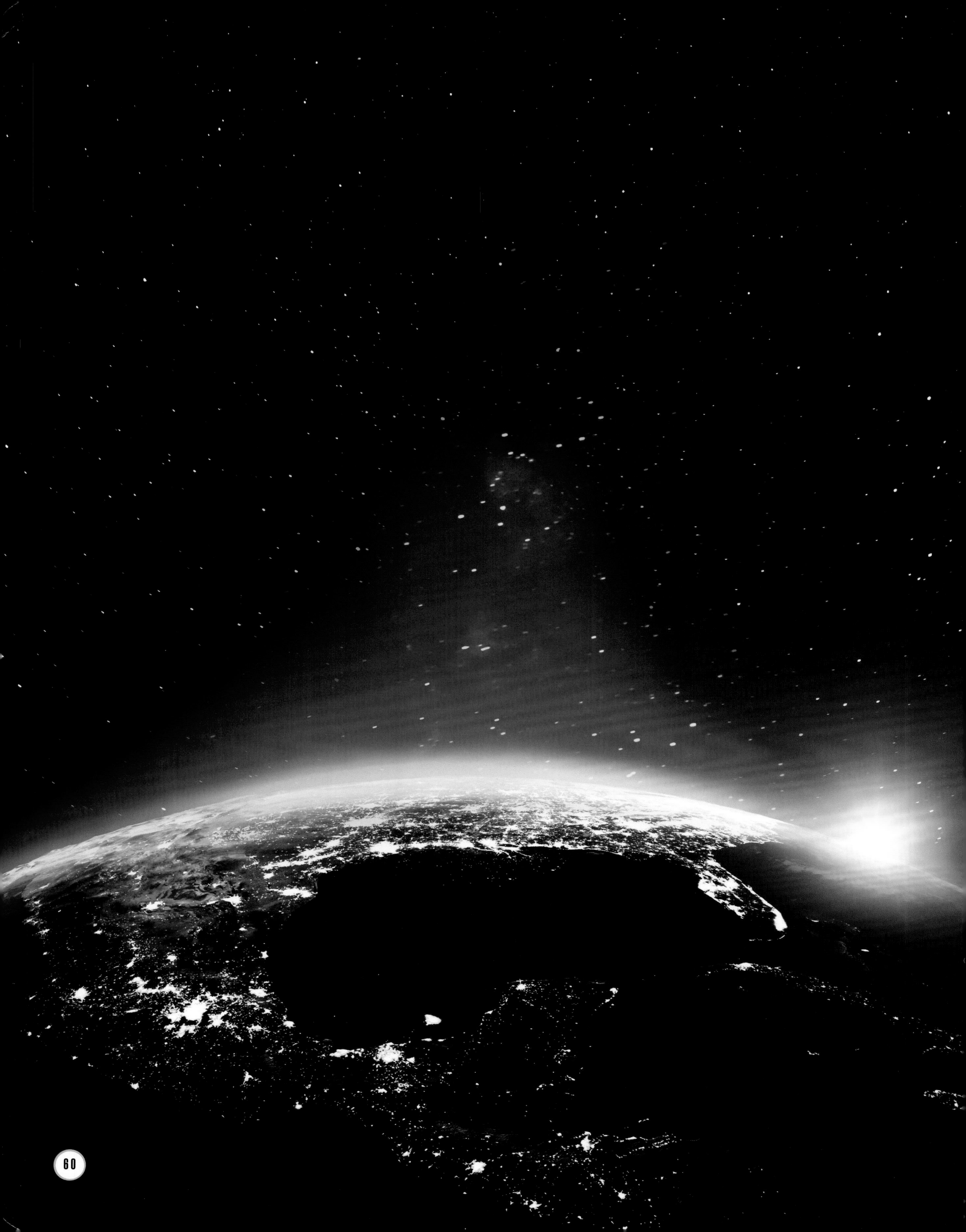